Simple

Pasta

Marilyn Bright

ILLUSTRATED BY CARL MELEGARI

KEY PORTER BOOKS

First Published in 1992 by
The Appletree Press, Ltd
19–21 Alfred Street, Belfast BT2 8DL
Copyright © 1992 The Appletree Press Ltd

Published in Canada by:

Key Porter Books Ltd
70 The Esplanade
Toronto, Ontario
Canada M5E 1R2

Canadian Cataloguing in Publication Data

Bright, Marilyn
Perfectly simple pasta

ISBN: 1-55013-418-1

| 1. Cookery (Pasta) | I. Title. | II. Series. |
| TX809.M17B75 1992 | 641.8'22 | C92-094518-X |

Printed in the E.C.

92 93 94 95 96 5 4 3 2 1

Introduction

Did Italian explorers discover pasta in China, or did Marco Polo merely report finding Chinese pasta "like ours"? The controversy continues, but the glories of fresh pasta have been rediscovered and have spread far beyond the shores of Italy and China. Recent dietary trends towards higher fiber and carbohydrate intake have rehabilitated pasta with a positive health image. New generations of cooks have turned to fresh home-made pastas and added their own variations to old traditions.

Fresh vegetables, meat, and fish team up with inventive sauces; old recipes are given twentieth-century updating with ingredients that might have startled Mrs Beeton, the Victorian cookery writer. At the same time, combinations such as pasta, tomatoes, and cheese never lose their charm – simply because they taste so nice together.

Being agreeably inexpensive in itself, good pasta deserves the best of accompaniments – good olive oil, fresh herbs and, most importantly, good cheese. Take a vow to avoid the pregrated stuff and treat yourself to the joys of fine cheese freshly grated over hot pasta. With a little butter and freshly-milled black pepper, such simple fare is the food of kings.

Most of the recipes in this little book are quite flexible, and the types of pastas indicated are often interchangeable, according to the cook's fancy. Unless otherwise indicated, *al dente* cooking of pasta is preferred; that is, pasta cooked not totally soft, but with some resistance "to the tooth".

Béchamel Sauce

Delicately-flavored white sauce, or *béchamel*, is used in many of the baked pasta dishes and is the versatile base for a classic cheese sauce.

4 tbsp butter
¹/₃ cup flour
2 cups milk
salt
freshly-grated nutmeg

Melt butter over low heat, stir in flour and cook for 1 minute. Gradually add milk and continue to stir over heat until mixture is smooth and thickened. Season to taste with salt and nutmeg. If sauce is not to be used immediately, cover surface with a buttered parchment paper to prevent skin from forming.

Cheese Sauce

Stir 1 cup grated cheese into the thickened *béchamel* sauce while it is still hot. A pinch of mustard powder may be added.

Sauce Napoli

Fresh-flavored tomato sauce and pasta is a gastronomic partnership that has survived the test of time, travelling from the Mediterranean to nearly every corner of the globe. Unless you have a source of homegrown sun-ripened tomatoes, the canned Italian kind are the best to use.

2 tbsp olive oil
1 onion, finely chopped
2 cloves garlic, finely chopped
2 x 14oz cans chopped tomatoes
1 tsp sugar
2 tbsp tomato purée
2 tsp dried oregano
salt and freshly ground black pepper
fresh basil leaves to garnish (optional)

Heat the oil and gently sauté the onion and garlic until soft. Add the remaining ingredients, cover and cook for 20 to 30 minutes, or until sauce is slightly thickened. Serve over hot pasta with fresh basil leaves strewn on top.

Bolognese Sauce

Known as *ragu* in its native Italy, this rich, meaty sauce is a classic served with spaghetti, or layered between tender leaves of baked lasagna.

3 tbsp olive oil
1 onion, finely chopped
1 carrot, finely chopped
1 clove garlic, finely chopped
1 stick of celery, finely chopped
3oz streaky bacon, finely chopped
8oz lean minced beef
$^1/_2$ cup red wine
14oz can of tomatoes
1 cup stock
1 tbsp tomato purée
freshly-grated nutmeg
salt, freshly-ground black pepper

Heat the oil and gently cook the onion, carrot, garlic and celery until softened. Add the bacon and the minced beef and stir over medium heat until evenly browned. Add wine, tomatoes, stock, purée, and a little grated nutmeg. Cover the pan and simmer gently for 30 to 40 minutes, adding a little water if mixture starts to stick. Taste and add salt, if needed, and black pepper.

Fresh Egg Pasta

Homemade pasta is a special gourmet treat, with greater flavor than the store-bought variety. In addition to cooking in a quarter of the time, it opens new possibilities for the cook's creativity with fillings and artistic shapes. Strong flour of the sort used for bread making is recommended for hand-rolled pasta.

4 cups flour
1 tsp salt
4 large eggs
6–7 tbsp water

Sift flour and salt into a large bowl and make a well in the center. Break eggs into the well and gradually stir the flour and eggs together, adding water in small amounts as necessary to make a soft dough. Form dough into a ball and knead on a floured surface until it feels firm and elastic, about 10 minutes. Divide dough into 2 or more pieces and, on a floured surface, roll each out as thinly as possible; the grain of a wooden table should be visible through it. Leave rolled sheets to dry for 30 minutes, then roll up in a scroll and cut into strips of the width desired, or cut into other shapes. Spread cut pasta on a cloth or on improvised racks to dry until required for cooking.

Maccheroni alla Carbonara

Delicious pasta, traditionally made by charcoal makers, carbonara is the perfect quick meal, using ingredients most likely to be at hand. Romans, who claim invention of this dish, most often use macaroni or thick-ribbed rigatoni, but Spaghetti Carbonara has become an international favorite.

4oz ham or bacon
1 tbsp butter
14oz macaroni or spaghetti
2 large eggs, beaten
$^2/_3$ cup grated Parmesan cheese
freshly-ground black pepper

Cut the ham or bacon into matchsticks and fry in the butter. Cook macaroni or spaghetti in plenty of boiling salted water; drain, and put into a heated dish. Quickly stir the eggs into the cooked bacon and pour the mixture over the hot pasta. When everything is well mixed, stir in the Parmesan cheese, reserving some to serve separately. Season well with black pepper and serve hot.

Pasta Baked with Mushrooms

Dried ceps, *trompettes-des-maures*, or your favorite wild mushrooms add special flavor to this vegetarian main-course dish. It can be assembled in advance, ready to slide into the oven when needed.

🐚

1oz dried wild mushrooms
2 tbsp butter
4oz fresh mushrooms, sliced
4 scallions, finely chopped
1¹/₂ cups béchamel *sauce*
approx. 3 cups pasta shapes, such as shells or bows
salt, pepper
¹/₂ cup grated cheese
finely chopped parsley to garnish

Preheat oven to 350°F. Soak the dried mushrooms in hot water until soft, then drain and chop coarsely. Melt butter and cook fresh mushrooms until soft, then stir in scallions and soaked dried mushrooms and cook for an additional minute. Remove from heat and stir in *béchamel* sauce. Cook pasta shapes in boiling, salted water until just slightly underdone. Drain and combine with mushroom sauce. Season to taste with salt and pepper, then turn into a greased baking dish and sprinkle cheese on top. Bake in oven for about 30 minutes, or until pasta is heated through and top is golden brown. Serve garnished with parsley.

Pasta Primavera

Tender, young vegetables lend springtime color to pale green pasta ribbons in a simple wine-and-cream sauce. The vegetables can be varied according to what is in season.

2 carrots
4 scallions, shredded lengthwise
6oz fresh asparagus
3oz mangetout
4 tbsp dry white wine
1 cup heavy cream
12oz green fettucine or tagliatelle
salt, pepper

Cut carrots into thin matchsticks. Cut shredded onions and asparagus into similar lengths. Blanch vegetables in a small amount of boiling water for 2 to 3 minutes, or until just *al dente*. Drain and set aside. Put wine into a saucepan and quickly reduce by half. Reduce heat and pour in cream to thicken gently while pasta is cooking in boiling, salted water. When pasta is nearly cooked, stir blanched vegetables into cream sauce to heat through. Season and pour over drained, cooked pasta.

Tortelli Stuffed with Spinach and Cheese

These delicious stuffed cushions of pasta are not beyond the abilities of novice cooks and well worth the time involved. Tortelli can be made early in the day, ready to be heated with butter and cheese, or baked in sauce when needed.

1 batch fresh egg pasta (p. 11)
Filling:
¹/₂ cup cooked spinach, drained and puréed
¹/₂ cup cream cheese
4 tbsp grated Parmesan cheese
1 egg, beaten
salt, pepper
freshly-grated nutmeg

Squeeze as much liquid as possible from the spinach, then combine with the cream cheese, Parmesan cheese, and enough beaten egg to make a soft paste. Season with salt, pepper, and grated nutmeg. Roll pasta into two rectangles, slightly thicker than for tagliatelle. Working quickly, lightly mark one of the rectangles into 2-inch squares. Place a teaspoonful of filling in each square. Use water or the leftover beaten egg to moisten along the scored lines with a pastry brush. Place remaining pasta sheet on top and press along cutting lines to seal well. Cut into squares and press edges again. Cook tortelli in boiling salted water, a few at a time, until they rise to the top, about 4–5 minutes. Serve hot with melted butter and grated cheese, or with prepared tomato sauce.

Pasta with Smoked Salmon and Dill Cream

Pale pink ribbons of salmon and green-flecked sauce inspire the cook to be art director. Choose butterfly or bow shapes, nests of fine-spun vermicelli, or tagliatelle in natural or green tints.

1 lb pasta shapes
³/₄ cup heavy cream
3oz cream cheese
2 tsp lemon juice
1 tsp anchovy paste
freshly-ground black pepper
6oz smoked salmon, thinly sliced
2 tbsp fresh chopped dill, or 2 tsp dried dill weed
dill sprigs to garnish

Cook pasta according to directions on package. Make sauce by gently heating cream with cream cheese, beating until smooth. Season with lemon juice, anchovy paste, and freshly-ground black pepper. Cut smoked salmon into ¹/₂-inch ribbons and stir into the sauce with the chopped dill. Drain pasta, stir in sauce, and transfer to heated dish. Garnish with dill sprigs.

Macaroni Vegetable Pie

Classic macaroni cheese becomes a party centerpiece in this vegetable-sparked version, which is topped with a golden-brown lattice of pastry.

8oz macaroni
1 tbsp olive oil
1 medium zucchini, sliced
1 onion, finely chopped
1 small red pepper, diced
1 cup canned corn kernels
1 clove garlic
1¹/₂ cups cheese sauce (p. 4)
3 tbsp parsley, chopped
6oz packet puff pastry
1 small egg, beaten

Preheat oven to 350°F. Cook the macaroni in boiling salted water until slightly underdone. Drain and set aside. Heat olive oil in a pan and stir-fry the zucchini, onion, pepper, corn and garlic until onion is slightly softened. In a large bowl, combine the cooked macaroni, vegetables, cheese sauce and parsley. Turn mixture into a greased ovenproof dish. Roll out puff pastry and cut into ¹/₂ inch strips. Lay pastry strips over mixture to form a lattice pattern and brush with beaten egg. Bake in oven until pastry is golden brown and pie is heated through, about 25 minutes.

Seafood Stuffed Pasta Shells

Large pasta shells filled with seafood make an eye-catching starter or main course for entertaining. The recipe is adaptable for fresh or canned fish according to the season.

12 extra-large pasta shells
1 tbsp butter
3oz mushrooms, finely chopped
4 scallions, finely chopped
2 cups flaked cooked salmon, crab or tuna
8–10 black olives, finely chopped
3 tbsp parsley, finely chopped
3oz cream cheese
lemon juice
salt and pepper
1 egg yolk
1 1/2 cups béchamel sauce (p. 4)

Preheat oven to 350°F. Cook pasta shells according to directions, drain and set aside. Heat butter and sauté the chopped mushrooms and onions until soft. Remove from heat and combine with the flaked fish, olives, parsley, and cream cheese. Season to taste with lemon juice, salt, and pepper. Stir in egg yolk and carefully spoon mixture into cooked shells. Arrange in greased ovenproof dish and spoon sauce on top. Bake in oven until shells are heated through, approximately 20 minutes.

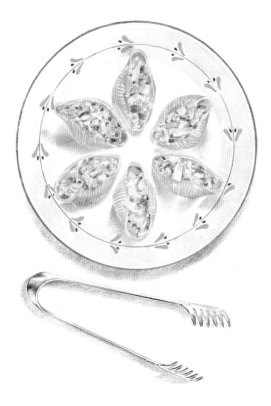

Ham and Leek Baked Lasagna

Precooked lasagna leaves have made easy work of layered pasta dishes. This creamy ham-and-leek version can be assembled a day ahead and refrigerated until needed.

❧

8oz cooked smoked ham, thickly sliced
2 tbsp butter
5 cups sliced leeks
3 3/4 cups béchamel sauce (p. 4)
2 cups grated mature cheddar
8oz lasagna leaves, pre-cooked type

Preheat oven to 350°F. Cut ham slices into 1/2-inch squares. Heat butter in a large pan and gently cook ham pieces with leeks until slightly softened. In a greased ovenproof dish, alternate layers of sauce, leek mixture, grated cheese, and lasagna until ingredients are used up. Finish with a cheese layer. Bake in oven for about 30 minutes, until golden brown on top.

Five-Pepper Pasta

The heat in this south-of-the-border sauce is determined by the type and quantity of chilli peppers used. Tiny red ones are usually the most incendiary, with pale green ones at the milder end of the heat spectrum.

1 red pepper
1 yellow pepper
1 green pepper
$^{1}/_4$ cup olive oil
3 tbsp tomato purée
1 ripe tomato, peeled, deseeded and chopped
1–4 chilli peppers, deseeded and chopped
1 clove garlic
lemon juice
salt
1 lb rigatoni
freshly-grated Parmesan cheese
coarsely-cracked black peppercorns

Broil the red, yellow, and green peppers just below the flame, turning frequently until the skin is blistered and charred. Rub off the skin and rinse, then deseed and cut peppers into strips. Put half the red pepper into a blender or food processor with the olive oil, tomato purée, chopped tomato, chilli peppers, and garlic, and process to make sauce. Season to taste with lemon juice and salt. Cook rigatoni according to directions on package, drain, and stir in pepper strips and sauce. Serve with Parmesan cheese and cracked peppercorns sprinkled on top.

Tuoni e Lampo

"Thunder and lightning" in English, this frugal Italian dish was traditionally made from the broken pasta at the bottom of the sack. This recipe uses chick peas but lentils, pinto beans, and other legumes make equally successful combinations.

8oz dried chick peas
2 tbsp olive oil
1 onion, chopped
1 clove garlic, crushed
sprig of fresh thyme
approx. 3 1/2 cups broken pasta or pasta shapes
Sauce Napoli *(p. 7)*
freshly grated Parmesan cheese

Soak chick peas overnight. The next day, heat olive oil in a large pan and sauté the onion and garlic until soft. Add chick peas and thyme and cover with water to a depth of 1 inch. Cook for 3 to 4 hours or until chick peas are tender and have absorbed most of their cooking liquid. Meanwhile, cook pasta, drain, and combine with hot chickpeas, adding salt to taste. Serve with Sauce Napoli and Parmesan cheese.

Vermicelli with Artichoke Hearts

Fine "angel hair" pasta makes an elegant starter or summer dish when swirled into nests with marinated artichoke hearts and dotted with toasted pine nuts. Substitute almond slivers if pine nuts are difficult to find.

1/2 cup olive oil
2 tbsp white wine vinegar
2 tbsp lemon juice
1 clove garlic, crushed
1 small chilli pepper, split
salt
14oz/396g can artichoke hearts, drained
12oz vermicelli
3 tbsp toasted pine nuts

Combine olive oil, vinegar, lemon juice, garlic, and chilli pepper in a small saucepan. Season with salt and heat gently without allowing to come to a boil. Remove garlic and chilli pepper and pour hot marinade over artichoke hearts. Set aside to cool. Cook vermicelli according to directions on package, taking care not to overcook. Drain pasta and toss in some of the marinade from artichokes. Swirl into nests on 4 serving plates, place artichoke hearts in the center and sprinkle with pine nuts. Drizzle a little more marinade on top and serve.

Spaghetti alle Vongole

Vongole are small clams that feature in this pasta favorite from the south of Italy. Other shellfish can be used, singly or in whatever mixture might appeal. Fresh mussels in their shiny black shells look particularly attractive.

3–4 lb fresh clams in shells
3 tbsp olive oil
1 small onion, finely chopped
2 cloves garlic, finely chopped
14oz can chopped tomatoes
$^1/_2$ cup parsley, finely chopped
14oz spaghetti

Scrub shellfish and rinse under running water to remove grit. Steam in a closed pan over hot water until shells open, about 5 to 8 minutes; discard any that remain closed. Heat oil and gently sauté onion and garlic until softened, then stir in tomatoes and cook until sauce is slightly thickened. Stir in opened shellfish and parsley and pour over spaghetti, which has been cooked *al dente*.

Classic Cannelloni

Creamy tubes of pasta bake in a golden covering of sauce in this Italian classic. Pre-cooked cannelloni tubes may be used but the dish must be baked and served right away or the shapes may burst. With conventional pasta, the dish may be assembled in advance and baked later.

8oz lean ground beef
4oz sausage meat
2 cloves garlic, finely chopped
approx. ³/₄ cup ricotta or cream cheese
1 small egg
bread crumbs
salt, pepper
12 cannelloni tubes
Sauce Napoli (p. 7)
béchamel sauce (p. 4)
freshly-grated Parmesan cheese

Preheat oven to 350°F. Fry the ground beef, sausage meat, and garlic together until meat is lightly browned. Drain off fat and combine meat with the ricotta (or cream cheese) and egg. Mix in enough bread crumbs to make manageable stuffing. Correct seasoning with salt and pepper. Cook cannelloni according to directions on package, until slightly underdone. Fill tubes with stuffing mixture and lay greased ovenproof dish. Pour Sauce Napoli evenly over cannelloni, then top with a layer of *béchamel* and sprinkle with Parmesan cheese. Bake in oven until golden brown and bubbling, about 45 minutes.

Pasta Shells with Blue Cheese and Walnuts

Any sort of pasta can be used in this recipe, but shell shapes hold more of the delicious creamy sauce. Gorgonzola, Stilton, Danish Blue, or Roquefort are just some of the many cheeses that are suitable.

🌰

10oz medium pasta shells
$^1/_3$–$^1/_2$ cup heavy cream
5oz blue cheese, crumbled
4 tbsp grated Parmesan cheese
freshly-ground black pepper
$^3/_4$ cup walnuts, coarsely chopped

While pasta shells are cooking, heat cream with blue cheese and Parmesan cheese, blending until smooth. Season with black pepper, add walnuts and pour over hot cooked pasta.

Rigatoni with Olive and Tuna Sauce

Tuna and tomatoes team up to make a quick main-course pasta dish that is perfect for busy day meals or unexpected visitors.

14oz rigatoni
2 tbsp olive oil
1 clove garlic, crushed
2 large tomatoes, peeled and chopped
1 tbsp tomato purée
25 stuffed green olives
6$\frac{1}{2}$oz can of tuna, well drained
freshly-ground black pepper

While rigatoni is cooking, combine olive oil, garlic, tomatoes, tomato purée, and olives in a blender or food processor and process briefly. Heat sauce with flaked tuna, season with black pepper, and pour over hot pasta.

Chicken Tetrazzini

Despite the Italian-sounding name, this dish appears to have originated in America. It is a good buffet dish, amenable to being made in quantity for entertaining.

10oz spaghetti
2 tbsp butter
8oz mushrooms, sliced
2 stalks celery, thinly sliced
5 scallions, chopped
4 tbsp flour
1 cup chicken stock
1 cup cream
3 cups diced, cooked chicken meat
freshly-grated Parmesan cheese
1/4 cup slivered almonds

Preheat oven to 350°F. Cook spaghetti *al dente*. Melt butter and sauté mushrooms, celery, and scallions until softened. Stir in flour and add chicken stock. Continue stirring until liquid is smooth and slightly thickened. Add cream and allow to thicken before stirring in chicken. Combine chicken and sauce with cooked spaghetti and transfer to greased ovenproof dish. Top with grated Parmesan cheese and slivered almonds and bake in oven for about 30 minutes until brown on top.

Seafood Pasta Bake

Mixed colors of pasta shapes or noodles can look very good in this delectable seafood main course. The relative amounts of white fish and more expensive shrimps can be adjusted according to the occasion and the state of the budget. Serve with a crisp salad and crusty bread.

1 cup cooked smoked haddock, flaked
1 cup cooked white fish, flaked
1 cup shelled cooked mussels
1 cup shelled cooked shrimp
2 tsp chopped fresh dill or 1 tsp dried
1 1/3 cups béchamel sauce (p. 4)
salt, black pepper
2–3 tsp lemon juice
approx. 3 1/2 cups cooked pasta
4 tbsp buttered bread crumbs

Preheat oven to 375°F. Check cooked fish for bones and skin, then combine with mussels, dill, and *béchamel* sauce. Season to taste with salt, pepper, and lemon juice. Stir cooked pasta into seafood mixture and turn into well-greased ovenproof dish; top with bread crumbs. Bake in oven until bubbling hot and golden brown on top, about 25 minutes.

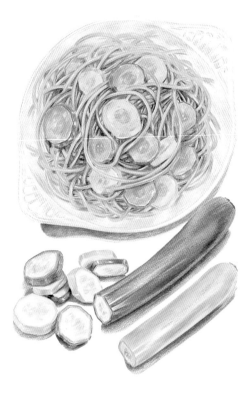

Spaghetti con Zucchini

The goodness of simple things is highlighted in this simple dish from the south of Italy. It looks especially inviting when made with a mixture of yellow and green zucchini. A simple dish like this deserves the very best fresh Parmesan cheese, hand grated just before using.

1 lb small zucchini
salt to sprinkle
14oz spaghetti
1¹/₂ tbsp butter
1¹/₂ tbsp olive oil
freshly-ground black pepper
fresh Parmesan cheese

Wash and slice zucchini, sprinkle with salt, and place in a colander to drain for about 45 minutes. When ready, rinse zucchini in cold water, drain, and press dry in a dish towel. Put spaghetti to cook in salted boiling water. Heat butter and olive oil together in a pan and gently cook zucchini until soft. Drain cooked spaghetti and toss in cooked zucchini. Season well with black pepper and serve with freshly grated Parmesan cheese.

Smoked Salmon and Pasta Salad

Elegant *roulades* of smoked salmon top pale green pasta salads for an unusual dinner-party starter. Like the other best-behaved dishes for entertaining, it is mostly done in advance and assembled just before serving.

❧

²/₃ cup heavy cream
3 tbsp bottled horseradish sauce
1 tbsp parsley, finely chopped
1 tbsp snipped chives
salt, pepper
8oz smoked salmon, thinly sliced
8oz green tagliatelle or fettucine
olive oil
mixed green salad leaves (lambs' lettuce, arugula,
endive, chicory, etc.)
lemon juice

Whip cream until very stiff, then fold in horseradish sauce, parsley, and chives. Season with salt and pepper. On a large piece of foil or wax paper, lay out slices of smoked salmon, overlapping pieces as necessary to form several rectangles. Spread the creamed mixture over the smoked salmon in an even layer and roll up carefully. Wrap rolls in plastic wrap or foil and place in refrigerator to chill. Cook tagliatelle, drain, and toss in a little olive oil to prevent sticking. Leave to cool. Arrange salad leaves on individual serving plates and make a nest of tagliatelle in the center. With a sharp knife, cut the chilled smoked salmon rolls into slices and place several pieces on top of each pasta salad. Just before serving, dress salads with a little olive oil and lemon juice.

Green Bean and Pasta de Luxe

Swiss cheese, pasta, and creamy sauce dress up green beans for serving as a vegetarian main course or along with plain grilled steaks or chops. Summer savory is the classic bean herb, and it is sold dried if fresh savory isn't available.

❦

8oz pasta bows, shells, or other shapes
8oz thin green beans
2 tbsp butter
2 tbsp onion, very finely chopped
2 tbsp flour
³⁄₄ cup commercial sour cream
1 tsp fresh summer savory, chopped (¹⁄₂ tsp dried)
salt, pepper
4oz Swiss Emmenthal cheese, shredded

Cook pasta until just *al dente*. Blanch green beans in boiling salted water for 3 to 5 minutes until cooked but still crisp; drain and set aside. Melt butter over low heat and cook onion until soft. Stir in flour, cook for 1 minute, then stir in sour cream. Season with summer savory, salt, and pepper, and cook briefly without allowing to boil. Combine sauce with blanched green beans and pasta and turn into greased flameproof dish. Top with Swiss cheese and broil until cheese melts and starts to turn color. Serve immediately.

Coronation Pasta Salad

Delicate curry and chutney seasonings make an appealing main course for summer. This is easy and economical to make in quantity for buffet entertaining.

꧁

2 tbsp dry sherry
about 2 cups cooked chicken, diced
³/₄ cup good commercial or homemade mayonnaise
4 scallions, finely chopped
1 tsp tomato purée
1 tsp lemon juice
¹/₂ tsp curry powder
2 tbsp apricot chutney
salt
approx. 3 cups cooked pasta shapes
chicory leaves
toasted flaked almonds

Sprinkle sherry over cooked chicken and set aside. Combine mayonnaise with onions, tomato purée, lemon juice, curry powder, and chutney. Taste, and salt if necessary. Stir together the sherried chicken, sauce, and pasta. Arrange chicory leaves in a circle on a large platter, spoon salad mixture into center and sprinkle with toasted almonds.

Chinese Beef and Noodle Stir-Fry

Chinese egg noodles are the ones sold in sheets like bits of ravelled knitting. They are generally steeped, or only briefly cooked, in boiling water. As in all stir-frying, the success of this dish depends on quick cooking over fierce heat.

🦂

12oz rump steak
1 clove garlic, crushed
1 tbsp soy sauce
1 tbsp brown sugar
1 tbsp dry sherry
6oz Chinese egg noodles
peanut oil
6 scallions, sliced
1 sweet red pepper, cut into strips
sesame oil

Semifreeze beef, then slice into paper-thin strips. Make marinade of garlic, soy sauce, sugar, and sherry, then stir into sliced beef and leave for 1/2 an hour. Cook egg noodles according to directions on package and drain. Heat peanut oil in wok or deep frying pan and quickly stir-fry the beef, which has been drained of marinade. Put beef aside and stir-fry noodles for a few minutes, then add scallions and pepper strips. Return beef to wok with other ingredients and cook all together for a minute. Sprinkle with sesame oil and serve immediately.

Pasta Cheese Ring

This baked pasta shape is designed to hold your choice of fresh cooked vegetables in a cream sauce, or simply buttered and seasoned. Mushrooms, baby spring vegetables, or brussel sprouts in cheese sauce are a few successful options.

8oz green or white tagliatelle
2 eggs, separated
1/2 cup milk
1 tbsp butter, melted
1/2 cup sharp cheddar, grated
pinch of salt
a little nutmeg, grated

Preheat oven to 350°F. Cook tagliatelle and drain well. Beat together the egg yolks, milk, melted butter, cheese, salt, and nutmeg. Combine with the cooked pasta. Beat the egg whites until stiff but not dry and fold into pasta mixture. Spoon into a well-greased 7-inch ring mould. Set mould into a shallow pan of hot water and bake until set, about 35 minutes. Turn out onto hot dish and serve filled with creamed vegetables.

Pasta Piedmontese

The quick and flavorful sauce for this garlic-lovers' treat has its origins in *bagna cauda*, the "hot bath" dipping sauce from the Piedmont region of Italy.

3oz fresh green beans
1/2 cauliflower, broken into small florets
2 large carrots, cut into thin matchstick-size pieces
4 tbsp butter
3 cloves garlic, crushed
8 anchovy fillets, drained
5 tbsp olive oil
12oz tagliatelle

Break the trimmed green beans into bite-size lengths and cook in boiling salted water with cauliflower and carrot sticks for 4 to 5 minutes, or until just lightly cooked. Drain and put aside. To make sauce, melt butter in a pan with garlic and cook gently for a minute. Add anchovies and mash to break them up. Add olive oil and keep hot while tagliatelle is cooking in boiling salted water. When pasta is cooked, stir prepared vegetables into hot sauce and pour over drained tagliatelle.

Index